Contents

 5A Assessment

Dreamer
page 2

 **5B Assessment**

The Cliff Track
page 14

Series editor **Dee Reid**

Part of Pearson

Characters

Anna

Anna's dad

Miss Smith

Tom

Talent show judge

Tricky words

- something
- sure
- listening
- watching
- quiet
- angrily

Read these words to the student. Help them with these words when they appear in the text.

Introduction

Anna lived in Aspen Road with her dad. She was a really good singer. She liked to sing at school and even at home when she was helping her dad with his work. Her dad had a dream that Anna would go on a TV talent show, but was that Anna's dream too?

Dreamer

Anna really liked singing
and she was a good singer.
At school she liked to sing with her friends.
At home, she even liked singing when she
was helping her dad with his work.

One night, Anna's dad saw something on TV.
"Look Anna," he said. "You should go on this.
You're really good at singing!"
But Anna wasn't sure she wanted to go on TV.

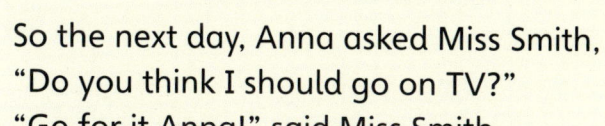

So the next day, Anna asked Miss Smith,
"Do you think I should go on TV?"
"Go for it Anna!" said Miss Smith.
"Everyone likes listening to you sing!"

But Anna still wasn't sure about being on TV.
So she asked her friend Tom.
He said, "You're a really good singer but
do you want to sing on TV?"

"I don't really want to," said Anna, "but my dad really wants me to sing on TV. It's his dream."

Weeks later, Anna went on TV.
Her dad and all her friends were
watching at home.

The music played and Anna started to sing.
Everyone liked Anna's singing.
She was really good.

The judge said to Anna, "I really like the way you sing." Then he asked, "Have you always wanted to be on TV?"

Anna went very quiet.

Then she said, "I like singing. I sing all the time. But I really don't want to be a singer on TV."

The judge looked cross.
"Then why are you here?"
he asked, angrily.
Anna didn't know what to say.
She turned to leave.
But the judge called after her,
"So what is your dream, Anna?"

Anna turned to face the judge.
"That's easy!" she grinned. "When I grow up,
I just want to work with my dad!"

Quiz

Text comprehension

Literal comprehension
p3 Where did Anna like singing?
p4 What gave Anna's dad the idea that she should go on TV?
p5 Why did Miss Smith say Anna should go on TV?
p6 Why did Anna ask Tom what he thought?
p12 What is Anna's dream?

Inferential comprehension
p6 Why is Tom a good friend?
p10 Why did Anna go quiet?
p11 Why is the judge angry?

Personal response
• Do you think Anna should have gone on TV?
• Why do you think talent shows are so popular on TV?

Spelling challenge

Study these words for one minute. Then write them from memory.
Phonically regular

home   quick   high   wait   which

Irregular

does   won't   other   really   caught

Ha! Ha! Ha!

When is a car not a car?

When it turns into a garage!

Characters

Nick

A boy

Tricky words

- cycling
- dangerous
- Olympic Games
- haunted
- another
- voice
- scared
- screamed

Read these words to the student. Help them with these words when they appear in the text.

Introduction

Nick liked cycling. He liked to go out on his bike and cycle off-road. He didn't worry how dangerous it was. He wanted to ride in the Olympics so he went out on his bike all the time. But there was one track Nick hadn't tried because it was supposed to be haunted.

The Cliff Track

Nick really liked cycling.
He liked to go out on his bike and cycle off-road.
He didn't worry how dangerous it was.

Nick wanted to ride in the Olympic Games.
If he really tried, he knew he could do it.
He went out on his bike all the time.

There was only one track Nick hadn't tried.
That was the track on the cliff.
Nobody ever went cycling there.
It was dangerous because the track
ran very close to the edge of the cliff
and people said it was haunted.

One day, Nick was out on his bike.
He was looking for another track to ride.
He made his way to the start of the cliff track.

I don't believe it can be that dangerous, he thought. *That story about it being haunted is rubbish!* So Nick started to ride his bike along the cliff track.

Nick sped along the track.
The track ran very close to the edge of the cliff.

"So you want to ride in the Olympic Games?"
said a voice.
There was a boy cycling by the side of Nick,
and he was on a bike just like Nick's.
Where had he come from? thought Nick.
"That's right, I do want to ride in the Olympic
Games," said Nick.

"So did I," said the boy. "But I never did.
I didn't ride in the Olympic Games and
you won't ride in the Olympic Games,"
said the boy and he laughed.
Nick turned to look at the boy. As he did so…
the boy's face changed.
Nick was looking at a skull!

Now Nick was really scared.
They were too close to the edge.
Suddenly the boy turned his front wheel
right into Nick's.

"No!" screamed Nick as both the boys and
their bikes crashed over the cliff.

Now Nick haunts the cliff track, waiting for the next boy who wants to ride his bike in the Olympic Games.

Quiz

Literal comprehension
p17 Why had Nick not been on the cliff track before?
p19 Why did he decide to go on the cliff track that day?
p19 Why was it called the cliff track?
p19 How can you tell Nick is a good cyclist?
p22 Why does Nick scream?

Inferential comprehension
p16 What was Nick's dream?
p20 What are the clues that the other cyclist is mysterious?
p21 Why was the ghost cyclist determined to stop Nick competing in the Olympics?

Personal response
• Do you think Nick was brave to ignore the rumours about the cliff track being haunted?
• Do you think Nick will really haunt the cliff track?

Spelling challenge

Study these words for one minute. Then write them from memory.

Phonically regular

around   **started**   **shouted**   **children**

Irregular

wanted   **because**   **something**
worked   **stopped**   **great**

Ha! Ha! Ha!

How do you stop a dog that will chase anyone on a bicycle?

Take away his bicycle!